# Cornerstones of Freedom

# The Story of
# THE
# PONY EXPRESS

By R. Conrad Stein

Illustrated by Len W. Meents

 CHILDRENS PRESS, CHICAGO

Library of Congress Cataloging in Publication Data
Stein, R. Conrad.
    The story of the pony express.
    (Cornerstones of freedom)
    SUMMARY: A history of the Pony Express, that
memorable and remarkable institution which lasted only
a year and a half, put to death by the telegraph.
    1. Pony express—Juvenile literature. |1. Pony
express| I. Meents, Len W. II. Title. III. Series.
HE375.P65S73        383'.143'0978        81-4558
ISBN 0-516-04631-4        AACR2
Copyright© 1981 by Regensteiner Publishing Enterprises, Inc.
All rights reserved. Published simultaneously in Canada.
Printed in the United States of America.
    3 4 5 6 7 8 9 10 R 91 90 89 88 87 86

WANTED—Young, skinny, wiry fellows not over 18. Must be expert riders willing to risk death daily. Orphans preferred.

This ad appeared in newspapers on the western frontier of the United States early in the year 1860. Hundreds of boys answered the help-wanted ad. They all hoped to become "pony riders." Orphans were preferred because riding for the Pony Express would be an extremely dangerous job. The company did not want to put up with grieving parents.

The Pony Express was born from a need to speed mail to California. A dozen years earlier, a California ranch foreman had seen a speck of gold shining in a river bed near Sutter's Mill. That first tiny speck of gold started a human stampede called the Great California Gold Rush.

In 1848 California was a sleepy territory. Only about 14,000 Americans had settled there. But by 1860, gold fever had brought nearly one-half million people to California. Most of the newcomers had come from the eastern half of the United States. All of them hungered for mail from their families and friends. But it took months for letters to cross the country. Also, in 1860 the United States was on the brink of civil war. Many people believed the war would be short. Californians were afraid it would begin and end even before they got the news that the first shot had been fired.

Before the Pony Express, the fastest way to move mail west was on John Butterfield's stagecoach line.

The famous "Butterfield Stages" carried mail, news dispatches, and passengers under a contract with the federal government. That contract required the stagecoaches to take the mail from Missouri south to the Mexican border at El Paso, Texas. From there they headed to San Diego. Finally they went north to San Francisco. It took the Butterfield Stages twenty-five days or more to reach San Francisco over this 2,800-mile route.

Sorting and delivering mail to scattered mining camps meant further delays. So when a homesick

San Francisco

Visalia

Los Angeles

Fort Yuma     Tucson

El Paso

Fort
Chadbourne

Fort
Belknap

Tipton     St. Louis

Mem,

Fort
Smith

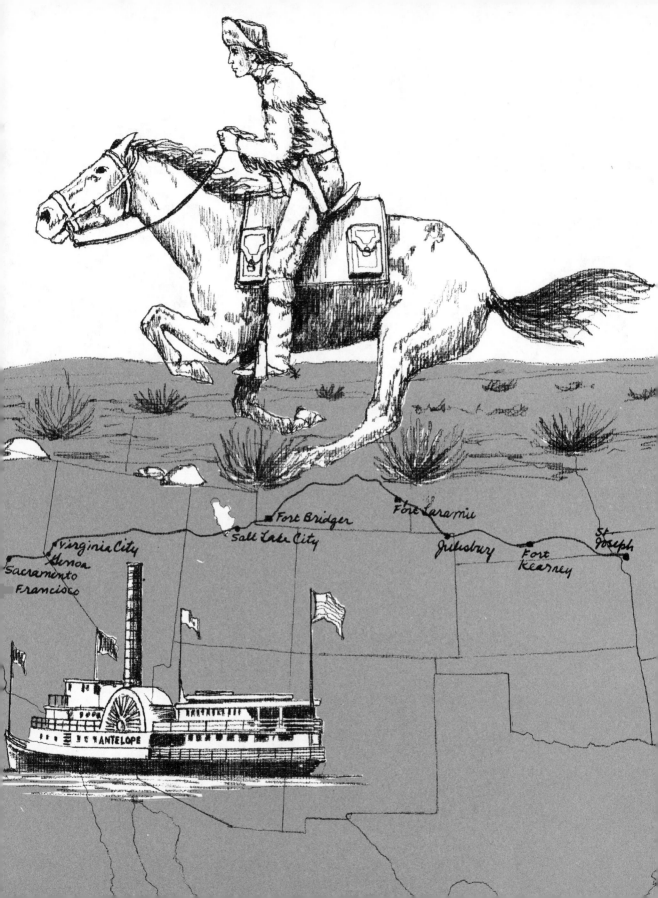

Fort Bridger

Fort Laramie

Salt Lake City

Virginia City

Genoa

Sacramento

Francisco

Julesburg

Fort Kearney

St. Joseph

ANTELOPE

gold miner finally did receive a letter from home, it was three or four months old.

There had to be a faster way to deliver mail. A man named William Hepburn Russell believed he knew a way. He felt that young men riding straight west on relays of fast horses could carry mail to California in just ten days.

Russell became the driving force behind the Pony Express. He was a sternly religious man. He believed that faith and hard work could accomplish anything. During the gold rush, Russell had earned a fortune in the stagecoach and shipping business. Now he hoped to earn another fortune by starting the Pony Express. He planned to open the company as a private mail service. Later he would try to secure a government contract.

Russell mapped out a trail from Missouri to Sacramento. From Sacramento, mail would be put on a steamer bound for San Francisco. Russell's trail stretched through 1,800 miles of western wilderness. Over that trail he built 190 stations. Next he bought horses, 500 in all. The cost of the project would be $100,000. Russell convinced his partners that the hoped-for government mail contract would more than repay the investment.

Finally, eighty young men were selected to race the mail across the continent. Russell gave each of them an engraved Bible. He made them swear, "I will, under no circumstances, use profane language; I will drink no intoxicating liquors; I will not quarrel or fight with any other employees of the firm ..." Some pretty rough characters worked for the Pony Express. Many of Russell's employees paid little attention to the vows they swore to uphold.

But they *were* devoted to their sworn duty of getting the mail through. The boy heroes of the Pony Express carried their mail over mountains and deserts, through mud, rain, sleet, and blizzards— and through the heart of hostile Indian country. Often the young pony riders had to defend their mail pouches with their lives.

Everyone on the western frontier was excited about the new Pony Express. Finally people in the West could enjoy a speedy mail service that would bring them both letters and news dispatches. A few days before the first run, a Kansas newspaper ran this huge headline:

**GREAT EXPRESS ADVENTURE FROM LEAVENWORTH TO SACRAMENTO IN TEN DAYS. CLEAR THE TRACK AND LET THE PONY COME THROUGH.**

At the time, telegraph wires stretched from New York City to St. Joseph, Missouri. This meant that truly important news could be wired from New York to St. Joe. From there, the Pony Express could hurry the news overland to Sacramento in ten days. To a Californian, that was a miracle.

## ST. JOSEPH

On the afternoon of April 3, 1860, hundreds of people gathered in St. Joseph, Missouri. A band played stirring music. The crowd cheered. And the very first pony rider galloped out of town carrying a mail pouch destined for California.

With all the fanfare and excitement that day, no one remembered to record the correct name of that first young pony rider. As a result, there was confusion over who it was. Some people said the first rider was Johnny Frey. Others claimed it was Bill Richardson, or Jack Keetley, or Don Rising, or Alex Carlisle, or one of the Cliff brothers—Gus or Charlie. Whoever he was, the rider raced out of St. Joe and into one of the most colorful chapters in the history of the United States.

At about the same time the first westbound rider left St. Joe, another pony rider rode out of Sacramento. He was headed east. The Pony Express was a two-way street, speeding mail across the country.

12

Ahead of those first riders lay a series of what were called *swing* and *relay* stations. Swing stations were spaced between fifty and one hundred miles apart. They were also called *home* stations because riders ate and slept there between runs. Relay stations were spaced just five to ten miles apart. The only function of a relay station was to provide fresh horses. To save time, the company allowed only two minutes for a rider to change horses. At the first sound of pounding hoof beats, or shouts from an approaching rider, the relay stationkeeper would saddle a fresh horse. In the station yard the rider leaped off his old horse, jumped onto the fresh one, and thundered away in a cloud of dust.

From the very beginning, the new mail service was a success. Racing from station to station, the riders accomplished exactly what the company advertised. They delivered mail across the western half of the country in just ten days.

Californians were overjoyed. The people of Sacramento greeted the first pony rider with a band that played "See the Conquering Hero Comes." One young Sacramento woman dashed up to the rider and tied her bonnet on his horse's head. That night crowds of people set bonfires in the streets. One bonfire was so big that the fire department was summoned. When the firemen were told that the fire had been lit to honor the new Pony Express, they dropped their hoses and joined the celebration.

Pony riders soon became heroes of the frontier. Poems and songs were written about their bravery. The riders loved the attention.

Most riders were boys in their teens. All were thin, because the company did not want them to weigh more than 130 pounds. The less weight a horse had to carry, the faster he could run. Riders received a salary of $125 a month plus bed and board. That was a fair wage, but Pony Express riders had to endure extreme hardship and danger.

The fierce weather of the western frontier was a constant enemy of pony riders. Sometimes a rider had to take his horse over desert sands under a blistering sun. At other times he had to force his way through blizzards and drifting snow. Often the snow was so deep it buried a horse up to the shoulders. On still other occasions a rider had to lead his mount gingerly over narrow trails that cut through the cliffs of the Sierra Nevada mountains.

Worse than the weather were the Indian wars that flared up on the frontier. When the Pony Express started, the western Indians were generally at peace with the settlers. Shortly after the first run, however, full-scale war broke out in what is now the state of Nevada.

In Nevada, Paiute Indians had seen miners kill their game, foul their streams, and take over land that had always belonged to the Indians. The Paiutes' frustration boiled over into war. They attacked all white settlements in their territory. Very often those white settlements were stations of the Pony Express.

A young rider named Nick Wilson became a veteran of the Paiute War when he helped two companions defend a station against an Indian attack. In the heat of battle, Wilson ran toward a large cedar tree. Suddenly he saw an Indian with his bow drawn back and an arrow pointed directly at him. The Indian fired. "The arrow struck," Wilson later wrote, "about two inches above the left eye." His two companions "tried to pull the arrow out, but the shaft came away and left the flint spike in my head." Because an arrow point was lodged in his skull, the two others left Wilson for dead. But after lying in a coma for eighteen days, he miraculously woke up. For years afterward, Wilson suffered from headaches. He wore a hat, even indoors, to cover the ugly scar on his forehead.

Despite the fury of the Indian uprising, Pony Express riders managed to get their mail through.

Stories about riders' dedication to protecting their mail were told from settlement to settlement. Pony rider Billy Tate, only fourteen years old, was caught in the middle of the Paiute War. He was killed in a battle, but he had put up a tremendous fight defending his mail pouch. The Paiutes so admired Tate's courage that they left the pouch untouched on his horse. Another rider was captured by a band of Indians who threatened to kill him. Luckily, one of the Indians had been a friend of the rider's father. He talked the other Indians into letting the man go. The rider, however, refused to go without his mail pouch.

The Indian wars caused drastic changes in the routes that had been so carefully laid out by the planners of the Pony Express. Some men had to ride double or even triple runs.

At the height of the Paiute War, Robert "Pony Bob" Haslam started out on his regular run in Nevada. Upon reaching his home station, Pony Bob discovered that his relief rider, afraid for his life, refused to mount up. Pony Bob decided it was his duty to carry the mail on another run. He reached the next home station, some 115 miles away, but his journey still did not end. The stationkeeper asked him to deliver the mail to yet another station farther up the trail. When he arrived, Pony Bob found the station house in flames.

The body of the stationkeeper was lying outside. The Paiutes had been there first. Pony Bob had no choice but to ride his horse to the next, faraway, home station. When he finally arrived there, he collapsed into bed. He had covered 384 miles on horse-back in thirty-six hours—all of it through hostile Indian country. Pony Bob had achieved a riding endurance record that would never be equaled in the history of the Pony Express.

The Indian wars cost the Pony Express the lives of seventeen of its employees. Most of the dead had worked in the stations. Manning a station was a less glamorous job than being a rider, but it was even more dangerous.

Some of the most famous men in the history of the American West worked for the Pony Express.

William F. "Buffalo Bill" Cody joined the Pony Express as a rider at age fifteen. In his autobiography, Buffalo Bill described riding furiously over the trail while being chased by Indians. Arriving at his station, he discovered "the stocktender had been killed there that morning, and all the stock had been driven off by Indians, and. . . I was therefore unable to change horses." So using his same exhausted horse, Buffalo Bill outraced the band of Indians to his next station.

Young Bill Cody rode for the Pony Express for about a year. When he quit, he became an Indian scout. Later, he became a buffalo hunter for the

railroads. Because he was such an efficient buffalo hunter, he earned the name Buffalo Bill. Regrettably, he was one of many men who took part in the destruction of the great buffalo herds that once roamed the plains. In his later years, Buffalo Bill owned a road show that staged Wild West acts. His most popular act showed a rider of the old Pony Express changing horses at a relay station.

WILD BILL HICKOK

James Butler "Wild Bill" Hickok worked for the Pony Express as a stationkeeper. While working for the company, he was involved in a bloody shoot-out with the notorious McCanles gang. Because he survived that shoot-out, he became known and respected as a gunfighter. Some years later, the people of Abilene, Kansas, asked Wild Bill to be their mayor. They hoped he could put an end to the drunken brawls between cowboys and railroad workers that raged on their streets. Hickok agreed, and though he preferred playing poker to breaking up fights, he did help bring law and order to the most lawless cattle town in the West.

It is said that the Pony Express gave birth to the doughnut. A famous rider, Johnny Frey, liked to eat sweet biscuits while racing his horse over his run. But Frey was so dedicted to speeding his mail from station to station that he could never spare the time to stop and pick up a biscuit at his girl friend's house. So his girl friend baked a biscuit with a hole in the middle. Then she stood on the side of the trail holding it out. Johnny Frey rode by, speared the biscuit with his finger, and carried it away without a pause. Thus the doughnut was born. At least that is the way the legend goes.

Certainly not a legend was a feared gunman named Joseph Alfred "Jack" Slade. He was a section boss in charge of several stations for the Pony Express. It was said that he shot men for simply looking at him the wrong way. The great writer Mark Twain once met Slade. Twain said in his book *Roughing It:* "He was so friendly and gentle-spoken that I warmed up to him in spite of his awful history." But when the writer and gunfighter drank coffee together, Twain reported, "The coffee ran out. At least it was reduced to one tin-cupful, and Slade was about to take it when he saw my cup was empty. He politely offered to fill it, but I... politely declined. I was afraid he had not killed anybody that morning, and might be needing diversion."

On the Pony Express, horses as well as men became heroes.

Most horses used by the company were mustangs that had been rounded up on the plains. They were trained, or "broken," by professional cowboys. One pony rider wrote that as soon as a cowboy "could lead them in and out of the stable without getting his head kicked off, they were considered broke..." Although they could be ornery, those tough mustangs made perfect mounts for pony riders.

24

Some of the horses seemed to be as dedicated to getting the mail through as the riders were. One story told of a rider who was killed during the Paiute War. Supposedly, he was picked off his horse by an Indian arrow. The riderless horse then galloped ahead to deliver the mail pouch to the next station. Once a jet-black mount called Black Billy brought an excited rider into a station. The rider said he had been attacked by Indians a few miles back. When the man dismounted, the stationkeeper discovered two Paiute arrows sticking out of the horse's flank. Black Billy was given tender care and a few weeks of rest before returning to his run. One morning a horse called American Boy broke away while the rider was changing horses at a relay station. Slung over the horse's empty saddle was the precious mail pouch. Several station hands chased American Boy, but could not catch him. It made no difference. The horse ran directly to the next station, dutifully delivering the mail.

Pony Bob claimed that he used his horse as a sort of radar system while traveling through Indian territory at night. "I kept a bright lookout," wrote the pony rider, "and closely watched every motion of my poor pony's ear, which is a signal for danger in Indian country."

During the Paiute War, Pony Express horses had a definite advantage over Indian mounts. Express horses were fed with grain. Indian horses ate only grass. Years earlier, the United States Cavalry had discovered that grain-fed horses can easily outdistance grass-fed horses. This knowledge saved the lives of many pony riders.

More important than most of the letters they delivered were the news dispatches Pony Express riders carried to isolated settlements in the West.

As the Civil War approached, frontier people first learned of Abraham Lincoln's election through dispatches carried by pony riders. In a record-breaking run of seven and one-half days, the Pony Express delivered Lincoln's inaugural address from Missouri to Sacramento. And pony riders also brought the news that all Americans dreaded to hear. A place called Fort Sumter had been fired upon and the United States had exploded into a bloody war.

Few other enterprises of the frontier captured America's imagination as did the Pony Express. Visitors to the West longed to see a young pony rider galloping break-neck over the trail, whooping and hollering as many of them did. While bouncing over a road in a stagecoach, Mark Twain was lucky enough to see a pony rider. He left us this stirring description:

HERE HE COMES!

  . . . Away across the endless dead level of the prairie a black speck appears against the sky, and it is plain that it moves. . . In a second or two it becomes a horse and rider, rising and falling, rising and falling—sweeping toward us nearer and nearer—growing more and more distinct, more and more sharply defined—nearer still, and the flutter of hoofs comes faintly to the ear—another instant a whoop and a hurrah. . . and a man and horse burst past our excited faces, and go winging away like a belated fragment of a storm!

The history of the Pony Express was glamorous but short. The service lasted only a year and a half. In that time the Express achieved all its goals save one. It never made a profit for its owners. In fact, by most estimates, Mr. Russell and his partners lost about $200,000 on the venture.

Initially, the Pony Express charged five dollars an ounce to deliver letters and news dispatches across the country. Although they earned some money, the cost of paying station men, paying riders, and buying new horses was too much for the company to bear. One of Russell's accountants wrote, "The amount of business transacted was not sufficient to pay one-tenth of the expense."

Also, the Pony Express never received the mail contract it had hoped to secure from Washington. Without government funds, the company could not continue.

The last blow came with the completion of the transcontinental telegraph which workmen had been constructing along the same route used by the pony riders. On October 18, 1861, the first message flashed over the new telegraph. Now news dispatches could be wired from coast to coast instantly. The newly completed telegraph was a competitor the Pony Express could never outdo.

On October 26, 1861, newspapers in the West reported:

## THE PONY EXPRESS WILL BE DISCONTINUED FROM THIS DATE.

During its short life the Pony Express delivered more than 30,000 pieces of mail. Remarkably, only one mail pouch ever was lost.

Although it lasted only a year and a half, the people of the West had fallen in love with their Pony Express. The day the company discontinued its service, a Sacramento newspaper called the *Bee* published this sad farewell: "Our little friend the pony is to run no more. . . . Farewell forever, thou staunch wilderness-overcoming, swift-footed messenger . . . . Rest on your honors; be satisfied with them, your destiny has been fulfilled—a new and higher power has superseded you."

The Pony Express was gone, but the boy heroes who risked their lives speeding mail over the wilderness will always be remembered.

About the Author

R. Conrad Stein was born and grew up in Chicago. He enlisted in the Marine Corps at the age of eighteen, and served for three years. He then attended the University of Illinois, where he received a Bachelor's Degree in history. He later studied in Mexico and earned a Master of Fine Arts degree from the University of Guanajuato.

The study of history is Mr. Stein's hobby. Since he finds it to be an exciting subject, he tries to bring the excitement of history to his readers. He is the author of many other books, articles, and short stories written for young people.

About the Artist

Len Meents studied painting and drawing at Southern Illinois University and after graduation in 1969 he moved to Chicago. Mr. Meents works full time as a painter and illustrator. He and his wife and child currently make their home in LaGrange, Illinois.